Hal Leonard Guitar
RECORDED VERSIONS™
With Notes & Tab

ERIC CLAPTON CROSSROADS VOL. 1

Transcriptions by Fred Sokolow

Cover and text illustrations by Ron Wood
Essay by Anthony DeCurtis

Hal Leonard Publishing Corporation

7777 West Bluemound Road P.O. Box 13819 Milwaukee, WI 53213

ERIC CLAPTON
A LIFE AT THE CROSSROADS

by Anthony DeCurtis

Over the past twenty-five years Eric Clapton's extraordinary career has traced a dramatic progression marked by musical pioneering, restless shifts of direction, spiritual awakenings, backsliding and, at one point, a total retreat into isolation. Clapton's mysterious, internally determined moves from budding pop star to purist blues man to rock guitar hero to laid-back troubadour have challenged the faithful and won new converts at every turn.

Through all the personal and artistic upheavals, part of Eric Clapton has consistently remained detached and calm, as if he accepted in his heart that he was destined for such shocks — and that acceptance brought a certain peace. At the same time he has maintained a fierce, private idealism about his playing. "My driving philosophy about making music," he told *Rolling Stone* in 1974, "is that you can reduce it all down to one note if that note is played with the right kind of feeling and with the right kind of sincerity."

It makes sense, then, that Robert Johnson's tough, transcendent masterpiece, "Crossroads," has become Clapton's signature song. On the path of life, crossroads are where the breakdowns and breakthroughs come, where danger and adventure lie. As he has forged and disbanded musical alliances, altered his sound and his look, pursued and dodged fame, Eric Clapton has brought himself to the crossroads and proven himself time and time again.

Clapton's bold search for his own identity is the source both of his enormous artistic achievement and his inner strife. That search acquired its momentum in the earliest years of his life. Clapton was born on March 30th, 1945 in Ripley, a small village about thirty miles outside — and a universe away from — London. His mother raised him until he was two years old, at which point she moved abroad, leaving him in the loving hands of her mother and stepfather.

The elderly couple was indulgent of Eric — they bought him his first guitar on an installment plan when he was in his teens — but the stigma of being born out of wedlock in a small town made a forceful impression on him. The "secret" of Clapton's illegitimacy was a secret only from him. "I was raised by my grandparents, thinking that they were my parents, up until I was nine years old," Clapton explained to J. D. Considine in *Musician* in 1986. "That's when the shock came up, when I found out — from outside sources — that they weren't my parents, they were my grandparents. I went into a kind of ... shock, which lasted through my teens, really, and started to turn me into the kind of person I am now."

Clapton was more pointed in Ray Coleman's authorized biography, *Clapton!*, published in 1985, about how hard it was to learn the truth about his background. "My feeling of a lack of identity started to rear its head then," he told Coleman. "And it explains a lot of my behavior throughout my life; it changed my outlook and my physical appearance so much. Because I still don't know who I am."

Like so many rockers, Clapton did a brief stint in art school — the Kingston College of Art, in his case. His formal education got derailed, however, when he was

about sixteen and began to make the bohemian scene in London, where he discovered folk-blues. Eventually he would go on to play acoustic gigs in coffee-houses and pubs, accompanied by a vocalist and doing tunes by Big Bill Broonzy, Ramblin' Jack Elliott and Blind Boy Fuller.

Another revelation struck around that time, as well. "Every Friday night, there would be a meeting at someone's house, and people would turn up with the latest imported records from the States," Clapton recalled in a 1985 *Rolling Stone* interview with Robert Palmer. "And shortly, someone showed up with that Chess album, *The Best of Muddy Waters*, and something by Howlin' Wolf. And that was it for me. Then I sort of took a step back, discovered Robert Johnson and made the connection to Muddy." In later days, Clapton would come to refer to Muddy Waters as his "father." And Johnson's haunted country blues affected Clapton so deeply that he would tell Dan Forte in *Guitar Player* more than two decades later, "Both of the Robert Johnson albums (*King of the Delta Blues Singers*, Volumes 1 and 2) actually cover all of my desires musically. Every angle of expression and every emotion is expressed on both of those albums."

The first band Clapton joined was the fledgling R&B outfit, the Roosters. The Roosters would last only a few months, from March to October of 1963, according to rock historian Pete Frame. But during that period the band's bassist, Tom McGuinness, who later played with Manfred Mann and McGuinness Flint, turned Clapton on to blues guitarist Freddie King's instrumental "Hideaway," and another influential figure entered Clapton's pantheon. Playing John Lee Hooker and Muddy Waters' tunes with the Roosters sharpened Clapton's playing, according to the band's pianist Ben Palmer, one of the guitarist's oldest friends. "It was immediately obvious that he was something that none of the rest of us were," Palmer says in *Clapton!* "And he had a fluency and command that seemed endless. The telling point was that he didn't mind taking solos, which people of our standard often did because we weren't up to it."

Following an extremely short stay with the pop band Casey Jones and the Engineers — headed by Liverpool singer Brian Cassar, who was trying to cash in on the record-company signing spree in the wake of the Beatles' success — Clapton joined the seminal Sixties band, the Yardbirds, in October of 1963. In their early days the Yardbirds — who, in addition to Clapton, consisted of vocalist Keith Relf, guitarist Chris Dreja, bassist Paul Samwell-Smith and drummer Jim McCarty — were an exuberant London R&B band that covered tunes like John Lee Hooker's "Boom Boom" and Billy Boy Arnold's "I Wish You Would."

On "I Ain't Got You" — and in his brief solo on the catchy New Orleans novelty, "A Certain Girl" — Clapton flashes the biting, fiercely articulate phrasing characteristic of his best playing. But in general Clapton was inhibited by the Yardbirds' harmonica-driven rave-up style. Despite his youth, Clapton was sufficiently confident of his musical tastes to become disgruntled when the Yardbirds, at the urging of manager Giorgio Gomelsky, edged away from the blues in order to pursue pop success. Clapton left the group by mutual agreement shortly after they recorded Graham Gouldman's "For Your Love" in quest of a hit.

Splitting from the Yardbirds on the brink of their commercial breakthrough was the first time Clapton displayed his willingness to pursue his own musical vision at whatever the cost — and it was far from the last. However high-minded and necessary such decisions were, Clapton is not beyond questioning them to a degree, in retrospect. "I took it all far too seriously," he states in *Clapton!* "Perhaps if I'd been able to temper it, I might not have been so frustrated . . . I still take it too seriously, in terms of relationships and being able to get on with other musicians. I'm far too judgemental, and in those days I was a complete purist. If it wasn't black music, it was rubbish."

Of course, seriousness about black music was hardly a problem during Clapton's tenure with John Mayall's Bluesbreakers in 1965 and 1966. A keyboardist with a vocal style derived from Mose Allison and Freddie King, Mayall was twelve years Clapton's senior and the father of the British blues scene. Mayall's Bluesbreakers were the proving ground for a host of ambitious young musicians in the mid to late Sixties, including Jack Bruce, Mick Taylor, Peter Green, Aynsley Dunbar, John McVie and Mick Fleetwood.

Clapton raided Mayall's vast collection of singles, and the two men thrived on each other's enthusiasm, as is evidenced by the raw Chicago blues power of their duet on "Lonely Years" and the spry assurance of their instrumental jam, "Bernard Jenkins." Though barely into his twenties, Clapton shaped an aggressive, tonally rich playing style with the Bluesbreakers. Drawing on Freddie King, Otis Rush and Buddy Guy in a way that blended respect with his own precocious mastery, Clapton unleashed some of the finest blues guitar playing of his generation on the 1966 *Bluesbreakers — John Mayall with Eric Clapton* LP. In addition, Clapton sang his first lead vocal on that record, a spare, eloquent reading of Robert Johnson's "Ramblin' On My Mind" that captures all that song's edgy amalgam of anguish and submerged threat.

Clapton's scorching club performances in London during his time with Mayall — represented in this collection by his ignition of Billy Myles' "Have You Ever Loved a Woman," with Jack Bruce on bass — quickly established a cult following for the young guitarist. "Clapton Is God" graffiti began appearing around the city, defining a central tenet of the Clapton mythology to this day. And though the comparisons with God would prove to be a hellhound on Clapton's trail, he understandably received the adulation more positively at first.

"My vanity was incredibly boosted by that 'God' thing," Clapton says in Coleman's biography. "I didn't think there was anyone around at that time doing what I was doing, playing the blues as straight as me. I was trying to do it absolutely according to its rules. Oh yeah, I was very confident. I didn't think there was anybody as good."

However appealing, the adulation did not prevent Clapton from taking a three-month break from the Bluesbreakers in 1965, and it was during that period that Jack Bruce joined the band. Playing with Bruce

upon his return spun Clapton's head around. Bruce's jazz background gave his playing an improvisational flair, and Clapton, who, despite his own purist impulses, had been feeling somewhat constrained in Mayall's strict blues format, felt a new sense of freedom. "Most of what we were doing with Mayall was imitating the records we got, but Jack had something else," Clapton told *Rolling Stone*, "he had no reverence for what we were doing, and so he was composing new parts as he went along playing. I literally had never heard that before, and it took me someplace else. I thought, well, if he could do that, and I could, and we could get a drummer . . . I could be Buddy Guy with a composing bass player. And that's how Cream came about."

Formed in 1966, Cream's impact on the world of pop music was immense. Rock bands to that point had played almost exclusively before crowds of screaming teeny-boppers — a major reason why live performance was beginning to seem pointless to bands whose music and ideas were becoming more sophisticated. Discussing rock and roll in musical terms was a joke to the mainstream media, and alternative media had not yet sprung up. Cream was a primary catalyst in transforming rock and roll into music that could be performed in concert before adults and analyzed with the same rigor that blues or jazz could be. The declaration implicit in the band's name was itself a demand to be taken seriously. In Coleman's terse summary, "They made musicianship hip." Clapton forever defined the role of guitar hero at this point, and with Bruce on bass and the redoubtable Ginger Baker on drums, Cream defined the power trio.

In their range and power, Cream forced a dichotomy between the studio and the stage. In the studio, the band was something like a later evolution of the Yardbirds. They could contain hip innovations within pop-song structures, as on "I Feel Free"; rework the blues, as on Willie Dixon's "Spoonful" and the Albert King-derived "Strange Brew"; journey into psychedelic wonderland, as on "Tales of Brave Ulysses" and "White Room"; or simply cut a radio-perfect, guitar-charged hit like "Sunshine of Your Love."

Live, however, Cream was essentially a rock-and-roll jazz band: Songs became thematic statements that provided the occasion for lengthy improvisational jams, with Baker and Bruce muscling each other into unexplored territory as Clapton wailed and roared above them. The propulsive live version of "Crossroads" included here is a Cream classic, and a masterpiece of concision — edited, as it was, by engineer Tom Dowd for the *Wheels of Fire* album — compared to the much longer renditions the band typically fired up.

The hero-worship Clapton had inspired when he was with the Bluesbreakers reached a fever pitch with Cream. The pressures of the inordinate praise heaped upon him, the wild improvisational competitiveness of Cream's gigs, and the fighting that resulted from Bruce and Baker's inability to get along gradually took their toll on Clapton.

"All during Cream I was riding high on the 'Clapton is God' myth that had been started up,"

Clapton told Robert Palmer. "Then we got our first kind of bad review, which, funnily enough, was in *Rolling Stone*. The magazine ran an interview with us in which we were really praising ourselves, and it was followed by a review that said how boring and repetitious our performance had been. And it was true! . . . I immediately decided that that was the end of the band."

Cream split up in November of 1968, about six months after that review appeared, and Clapton began jamming with Steve Winwood, the keyboardist and sterling R&B vocalist who had made his own youthful mark with the Spencer Davis Group and Traffic. The two men had played and recorded together two years earlier, and Clapton admired Winwood's tunefulness as a singer and songwriter — qualities that stood in sharp relief after the jazz-rock experimentalism of Cream.

But, given their musical pedigrees, Clapton and Winwood were hot commercial commodities. Because all three of its members had been eminent figures on the British scene, Cream had begun a trend toward supergroups, and the prospect of Winwood and Clapton teaming up was too hot a proposition for the business people to resist. What began idyllically with Clapton and Winwood jamming together at their homes in the country and searching for new musical directions quickly became a cash cow. Ginger Baker and Rick Grech, bassist of the English folk-rock band Family, were recruited as the rhythm section, and Blind Faith was born.

Formed in early 1969, Blind Faith debuted at a huge outdoor concert in London's Hyde Park in June of that year, recorded one album and then launched an arena tour in America. The band broke up in late 1969, and Clapton offered this bluntly honest obituary in *Rolling Stone* shortly afterwards: "We didn't rehearse enough, we didn't get to know each other enough, we didn't go through enough trials and tribulations before the big time came."

Still, the *Blind Faith* album, recorded in February, May and June of 1969 had a number of splendid moments. Steve Winwood's searching "Can't Find My Way Home," with Clapton on acoustic guitar, is a fine example of the kind of melodic, song-centered work Clapton was becoming more interested in after Cream. Among the earliest tunes Blind Faith laid down in the studio, Clapton's "Presence of the Lord" was the first non-instrumental song he ever recorded that he wrote fully on his own. It was also the first of the hymn-like spiritual songs of faith that would become a staple of his work in years to come.

The opening act on the Blind Faith tour of America in 1969 was a rocking R&B band led by Delaney and Bonnie Bramlett. Delaney and Bonnie played a loose, engaging blend of the full range of American soul music, and their unassuming, good-hearted shows seemed to Clapton a sharp contrast to Blind Faith's headline gigs. Clapton began spending more and more time with Delaney and his band, traveling from gig to gig on their tour bus and popping up on stage during their sets. In a 1970 interview in *Rolling Stone*, Clapton recalled that "on certain nights I'd get up there and play tambourine with Delaney's group and enjoy it more

than playing with Blind Faith . . . And by then I kind of got this crusade going for Delaney's group. I wanted to bring them over to England."

Blind Faith splintered once their blitz of America ended. At that point, Clapton not only sponsored a tour of England for Delaney and Bonnie, he played guitar with the band and recorded the infectiously upbeat single, "Comin' Home," with them. A live album from the tour was released later. More important, however, Delaney was the agent of a significant emotional breakthrough for Clapton.

Since about 1968, Clapton had been growing bored with virtuoso musicianship and more interested in songs that had clearly delineated structures and put across a pleasing groove. The Band's *Music from Big Pink*, which came out that year, made a striking impression on him and fueled his dissatisfaction with Cream. Discussing Cream's break-up in *Rolling Stone* in 1974, Clapton said "another interesting factor was that I got the tapes of *Music from Big Pink* and I thought, well, this is what I want to play — not extended solos and maestro bullshit but just good funky songs." The concise, melodic "Badge," which Clapton co-wrote for Cream's *Goodbye* album with George Harrison, who also plays guitar on the song, was one product of this interest. Forming a band with Steve Winwood and serving as a guitar-slinger side-man to Delaney and Bonnie were other manifestations of it.

Yet despite his strong performances on "Ramblin' on My Mind," "Crossroads" and other tracks, Clapton was still extremely shy about his singing. Clapton told Robert Palmer that on the night he and Delaney met, "Delaney looked straight into my eyes and told me I had a gift to sing and that if I didn't sing, God would take it away. I said, 'No, man, I can't sing.' But he said, 'Yes, you can.' . . . That night we started talking about me making a solo album, with his band."

When Delaney and Bonnie's tour of England ended, the two men went into the studio in Los Angeles and began work on Clapton's first solo album, *Eric Clapton*. Delaney's influence on the record was considerable. He produced the album — which includes the joyful "Blues Power" and the fiery "Let It Rain" — and supplied most of the players from his own band. His hand is especially evident on the alternative version of J. J. Cale's "After Midnight" — which Delaney mixed and which features a horn section that does not appear on the LP track. With Delaney's encouragement, Clapton emerged as a front man for the first time since he had been propelled into superstardom with Cream. Clapton wrote or co-wrote eight of the eleven tunes on the record, sang all the lead vocals and played crisply and spiritedly. He was now ready to put together a band of his own.

When Clapton learned that three members of Delaney's band — keyboardist Bobby Whitlock, bassist Carl Radle and drummer Jim Gordon — had had a falling out with their boss and were available, he scooped them up. The band came together and did their first recording while they were all working on the sessions for George Harrison's *All Things Must Pass* album, which Phil Spector was producing. They recorded a blistering version of "Tell the Truth" —

backed with the salacious "Roll It Over," featuring Harrison and Dave Mason on guitars — as a single, with Spector at the board. But, at the band's insistence, the track was recalled within days of its released.

Still ambivalent about his rock-star status, Clapton avoided using his own name and debuted his new band at a benefit concert in London as Derek and the Dominos. And rather than play large halls, he booked a club tour of England for their first trip out. As undisputed leader of the Dominos, Clapton was able both to play songs he felt comfortable with and to stretch out in solos when he desired. "It wasn't until I formed Derek and the Dominos and we played live that I was aware of being able to do exactly what I wanted and was happy with it," Clapton told Dan Forte in 1985. But Clapton's musical satisfaction contrasted with the emotional pain he was experiencing. He had fallen in love with Pattie Boyd Harrison, who at the time was married to his best friend, George Harrison. With the turmoil of a classic blues triangle worthy of Robert Johnson exploding inside him, Clapton left for Miami with the Dominos to make *Layla*.

Layla was recorded with legendary producer Tom Dowd under the most extreme conditions. Critic Robert Palmer visited the sessions and later recalled, "There was a lot of dope around, especially heroin, and when I showed up, everyone was just spread out on the carpet, nodded out." Shortly after the band arrived in Miami, Dowd took them to see the Allman Brothers, and Duane Allman was invited to play slide guitar on the album. Allman also teamed up with Clapton for a duet on Little Walter's "Mean Old World," which was not included on the LP.

Driven creatively by his new band, the formidable playing of Allman and his own romantic agony, Clapton poured all he had into *Layla*'s title track, which was inspired by a Persian love story he had read, *The Story of Layla and Majnun* by Nizami. The song's extended lyrical coda was composed independently by drummer Jim Gordon on piano, and Gordon had to be convinced to allow the piece to be tacked onto "Layla."

After completing *Layla*, Derek and the Dominos launched a tour of America, from which the previously unreleased live versions of "Key to the Highway" and "Crossroads" — in a more churning, exploratory rendition than the one recorded with Cream — included in this collection are taken. The band then returned to England, and in April and May of 1971 attempted to record a second studio album — five tracks of which are presented in this collection for the first time: "One More Chance," Arthur Crudup's "Mean Old Frisco," the instrumental "Snake Lake Blues," a cover of Willie Dixon's "Evil," and an uncompleted studio version of "Got to Get Better in a Little While," which the band performed live on the album, *Derek and the Dominos in Concert*. In his 1985 interview in *Rolling Stone* Clapton told Robert Palmer that the sessions for a follow-up LP to Layla "broke down halfway through because of the paranoia and the tension. And the band just . . . dissolved."

Once the Dominos broke up, Clapton's drug dependence worsened and kept him virtually a prisoner in his home for the rest of 1971 — though he did emerge to play at George Harrison's Concert for Bangladesh that summer — and much of the following year. During this period he felt both personally and emotionally adrift, and the long-standing identity issues arose once again. "The end of the Dominos came too soon, and that left me very high and dry as to what I was supposed to be," he told *Guitar Player* in 1985. "I'd been this anonymous person up until that time. It was difficult for me to come to terms with the fact that it was *me*, that I was on my own again."

Part of that difficulty may have resulted from the origins of Derek and the Dominos in Clapton's own psychic need. Despite the enormous satisfactions the band brought him, Clapton told *Musician* that Derek and the Dominos were "a make-believe band. We were all hiding inside it. Derek & the Dominos — the whole thing was . . . assumed. So it couldn't last. I had to come out and admit that I was being me. I mean, being Derek was a cover for the fact that I was trying to steal someone else's wife. That was one of the reasons for doing it, so that I could write the song, and even use another name for Pattie. So Derek and Layla — it wasn't real at all."

Clapton's good friend Pete Townshend of the Who organized a concert at London's Rainbow Theatre in January of 1973 to create some momentum for the guitarist's return to action. Clapton played at the highly emotional show with Townshend, Ron Wood and Steve Winwood, and later that year took an acupuncture cure

to end his drug addiction. Once that problem was behind him, Clapton contacted Tom Dowd and returned to Miami to record *461 Ocean Boulevard*.

Featuring a band of American musicians, including Carl Radle, brought together by Dowd, *461 Ocean Boulevard* is Clapton's great comeback LP. Appropriately, it opens with "Motherless Children," a traditional tune whose rollicking energy in Clapton's slide-guitar version counterpoints its relevance to the circumstances of his early life. The deeply felt "Let It Grow" finds Clapton once again "standing at the crossroads," and this time making a choice to affirm life, love and, by extension, his ability to reach within himself and create art. And *461 Ocean Boulevard* contained Clapton's cover of Bob Marley's "I Shot the Sheriff" — represented here in a tougher, more expansive live rendition from the band's December 5th, 1974 concert at the Hammersmith Odeon in London — which exposed millions of Americans to reggae music for the first time when it became a Number One hit. During the *461 Ocean Boulevard* sessions at Criteria Studios in Miami, Clapton also recorded Jimmy Reed's insinuatingly seductive "Ain't That Lovin' You" with Dave Mason on guitar — a previously unreleased track included in this collection.

461 Ocean Boulevard re-established Clapton in both critical and commercial terms, but it also ushered in the phase of his career that engendered concern in many of his longest-standing followers. In their concentration on songwriting, vocals and melody, *461 Ocean Boulevard* and the nine studio LPs that have followed it de-emphasize the pyrotechnic guitar work that characterized Clapton's tracks with the Bluesbreakers, Cream and Derek and the Dominos — though there's certainly no shortage of excellent playing. Working with a variety of producers — including Dowd, Glyn Johns and Phil Collins — Clapton alternated between American and British bands, experimenting with a wide variety of sounds and styles. Conventional pop songs and laid-back ballads of broad appeal appeared on those records and jarred the sensibilities of some fans.

A number of issues are important for understanding Clapton's music since 1974. One is that, while Clapton is still gripped by the blues and inclined to explore his favorite standards at length in live performance (note his probing reading of Otis Rush's "Double Trouble" in this collection), that impulse is no longer single and all-consuming. Since the latter days of Cream, the thrust of Clapton's music has been towards melody, and the artists that have interested him — the Band, Bob Dylan, Bob Marley, J. J. Cale, country singer Don Williams — are often more subtle than they are explosive. Taken together those artists and Clapton's blues idols are the influences behind his most notable work of the late Seventies and Eighties.

In 1985 Clapton spoke of a desire he felt during the Seventies "to be more of a composer of melodic tunes rather than just a player, which was very unpopular with a lot of people." The remark echoes something he said eleven years earlier, in expressing admiration for Stevie Wonder: "I think when it comes down to it, I always go for singers. I don't buy an album because I

like the lead guitar. I always like the human voice most of all." The greatest blues guitar playing, after all, is modeled on the sound of the human voice.

Blues, country, folk, rock and pop have come to share a place in Clapton's music. He offered a sensitive reading of Elmore James' "The Sky Is Crying" on *There's One in Every Crowd* (in addition to recording James' "(When Things Go Wrong) It Hurts Me Too" during the sessions for that album), and, in a live cut from 1977 included here, did an upbeat take on "Further On Up the Road," which over the years has become one of his signature tunes. Members of the Band were a prominent presence on the gently rolling *No Reason to Cry* album, which featured Clapton's optimistic "Hello Old Friend." Bob Dylan appeared on that record as well, sharing the vocal on his enigmatic song, "Sign Language."

Clapton also turned in fine versions of Dylan's "Knockin' on Heaven's Door" — another expression of the guitarist's spiritual side — and his swinging "If I Don't Be There By Morning." J. J. Cale's ominously enticing "Cocaine," included on Clapton's 1978 multi-platinum LP, *Slowhand*, has proven to be one of Clapton's most popular tunes, and Clapton's own catchy hit, "Lay Down Sally," from that same album, owes a clear debt to Cale. The affectionate "Wonderful Tonight," also from *Slowhand*, was simply born of Clapton's wish to write a love song.

Clapton's popularity as a live performer has consistently grown over the past ten years, and the videos and the pop-oriented LPs he has made with producer Phil Collins — *Behind the Sun* and *August* (which was co-produced by Tom Dowd) — have brought his music to a younger audience eager to learn about his past. He composed a soundtrack for the BBC television series *Edge of Darkness*, which won prestigious BAFTA and Ivor Novello awards in Great Britain, and for the film *Lethal Weapon*. He contributed songs to films, including "Heaven Is One Step Away" for *Back to the Future* and two tracks for *The Color of Money*, directed by Martin Scorsese.

As a blues prodigy, Clapton built a commanding reputation very early in his twenties. By the time he was thirty he had, like many masters, become intrigued by simplicity — the one-note philosophy. The calm that he felt at his core — through the times of revolutionary innovation, through the drugs and the cure, through heartbreak and happiness, at the crossroads and further on up the road — finally entered his music.

In *Musician* in 1986 Clapton said, "I think that the ultimate guitar hero should be a dispenser of wisdom, as well as anything else. . . . that's the one thing I will say that I'm still striving after, outside of perfection as a musician: the attainment of wisdom, in any amount."

If wisdom can be reflected in the creation of a superbly accomplished body of work and in the defeat of personal adversity, Eric Clapton has already achieved the major portion of his goal. And the remainder has not escaped him. It awaits him — and us, his audience — at the spectacular series of crossroads to come.

— Anthony DeCurtis
Senior Writer
Rolling Stone

ERIC CLAPTON'S GUITAR STYLE

by Fred Sokolow (Transcriber)

Clapton's main musical inspiration was the rich heritage of American blues guitar. Before he evolved his distinctive, recognizable style, he studied and emulated rural acoustic players like Robert Johnson, Skip James and Blind Boy Fuller, and artists with rural roots who made the transition to electric blues, like John Lee Hooker and Muddy Waters. His playing also reflected the fully realized electric blues techniques of guitarists like B. B. King, Buddy Guy, Otis Rush and Freddie King, and urban rhythm and blues players like Chuck Berry and Bo Diddley.

All these influences are heard in Clapton's playing throughout his career. In the first two albums of the CROSSROADS set (transcribed in this volume), you can hear how Clapton changed from an excellent imitative blues guitarist into an innovative, brilliant blues player with a distinctive style; and finally (with Cream and Blind Faith) he became an original, trailblazing rock guitarist who forever changed the sound of electric guitar music.

It didn't happen overnight. In the Yardbirds material, Clapton's tone was still developing and, for all his fluid dexterity, his playing was derivative. On A CERTAIN GIRL, I AIN'T GOT YOU and GOT TO HURRY he played through a tinny fuzztone — an early attempt to find a richer sound. The latter tune, an instrumental, gave him room to stretch out and display some blues chops. He was already playing all over the fretboard, using all the blues positions.

Some blues techniques Clapton employed with the Yardbirds have continued to be his trademarks through all phases of his career:

FIRST POSITION/E LICKS — In Hooker's BOOM BOOM, Clapton played standard first position/key of E licks á la Hooker, Lightnin' Hopkins and other Texas blues guitarists. For more of the same, see HIDEAWAY, RAMBLIN' ON MY MIND, SPOONFUL and SLEEPING IN THE GROUND.

BOOGIE BACKUP PATTERNS — Clapton backed up the vocals in I WISH YOU WOULD and A CERTAIN GIRL with single-note boogie lines. See BERNARD JENKINS, HIDEAWAY and ALL YOUR LOVE for more examples of this technique. In RAMBLIN' ON MY MIND he played a Lightnin'-style first position/E chord boogie line on the bottom bass strings and in FOR YOUR LOVE (during the bridge), LAWDY MAMA and CROSSROADS he played Chuck Berry-style moveable, double-note bass/boogie lines. Also notice his Berry-like double-note lead licks in HONEY IN YOUR HIPS, A CERTAIN GIRL and I AIN'T GOT YOU. His sliding chords in the Jimmy Reed tune BABY WHAT'S WRONG are reminiscent of Berry's famous MEMPHIS lick.

BACKUP RIFFS — Clapton played repetitious, bluesy backup riffs in BOOM BOOM and the bridge of I AIN'T GOT YOU. Later rock/blues tunes STRANGE BREW and SUNSHINE OF YOUR LOVE included similar backup riffs.

PLAYING IN A HIGH REGISTER — In his earliest recordings, Clapton played in all the moveable blues positions — he seldom stuck with the familiar first and second positions. This often took him to the last few frets of his guitar; see for example, whole sections of I AIN'T GOT YOU, GOT TO HURRY, ALL YOUR LOVE, HAVE YOU EVER LOVED A WOMAN, CROSSROADS and PRESENCE OF THE LORD.

SLIDE GUITAR — Clapton's bottleneck lead on GOOD MORNING LITTLE SCHOOLGIRL is in open E tuning. The next year (1965) he recorded LONELY YEARS bottleneck style, in open A tuning. He has often played slide guitar in open and standard tunings throughout his career.

When Clapton left the Yardbirds in 1965 he spent a month in seclusion immersing himself in blues guitar. Then he resurfaced in London and joined John Mayall and the Bluesbreakers and there was a dramatic improvement in his playing and his *sound*. On LONELY YEARS, the first recording with Mayall in this collection, Clapton captured the Muddy Waters finger-picking/bottleneck style. (Fingerpicking pops up on most of Clapton's Lps: see CROSSROADS, RAMBLIN' ON MY MIND and CAN'T FIND MY WAY BACK HOME for more examples.) Clapton's *tone* stood out — it was fatter, richer and warmer than before.

By the following year, when he recorded a supercharged version of the Freddie King instrumental HIDEAWAY and Otis Rush's ALL YOUR LOVE, Clapton had achieved a distinctive, powerful, unique sound. Most of the playing techniques and characteristics that made guitar history are featured in these and the other Bluesbreakers' selections:

TUBE DISTORTION — The rich, screaming, urgent tone of a guitar overdriving a tube amplifier — which ultimately became the archetypal rock guitar sound — had been used before Clapton as an effect, a novelty. He built a style around it. Unlike the grating fuzztone sound, Clapton's distortion was warm and full with a singing, sustaining vibrato and a feeling of limitless energy straining to be unleashed. The uniqueness of his tone was startlingly evident on ALL YOUR LOVE.

BLUESY VIBRATO — Clapton didn't invent left-hand vibrato, but this technique, coupled with overdrive/distortion, took on an exaggerated, sing-ing sound of its own. In enabled Clapton to sustain notes longer than usual because tube distortion plus good left-hand vibrato equals long decay.

SUSTAIN AND FEEDBACK — Sometimes, at peak volume, feedback occurs between amp speakers and guitar pickups. Clapton controlled feedback to swell and further sustain a note. Listen to ALL YOUR LOVE, HAVE YOU EVER LOVED A WOMAN and SPOONFUL for examples.

RADICAL STRING-BENDING — James Burton popularized the use of extra light strings; they helped him play string-bending licks to imitate a pedal steel. Clapton bent the strings further — one and a half, even two whole steps — to imitate a howling, swooping, soaring blues singer like Muddy Waters or Howlin' Wolf. He often bent the strings on a sustained note, with or without vibrato. For examples, see ALL YOUR LOVE, HAVE YOU EVER LOVED A WOMAN, RAMBLIN' ON MY MIND, WRAPPING PAPER, I FEEL FREE, SPOONFUL, SUNSHINE OF YOUR LOVE and STEPPIN' OUT.

When Clapton left the Bluesbreakers and formed Cream, he used all these techniques in a new context. The wah-wah pedal heard in TALES OF BRAVE ULYSSES and WHITE ROOM was the only new *effect*. But listen to I FEEL FREE to hear how fresh and new Clapton's string-bending, vibrato and overdrive sound outside of the blues mode. Even when he played a blues tune like SPOONFUL, he sounded like no one else.

There had been rock guitar heroes before Clapton; Chuck Berry and Bo Diddley were the first to hold the title. Clapton and Cream took the glorification of the guitar virtuoso a step further, allowing Clapton to play five- or ten-minute solos in SPOONFUL or the Robert Johnson tune, CROSSROADS. Clapton had the confidence to playfully quote the Rodgers and Hart standard BLUE MOON in the beginning of his solo to SUNSHINE OF YOUR LOVE, or to echo several bars of Albert King's solo (on OH PRETTY WOMAN) in his solo for STRANGE BREW.

You can hear Clapton growing as an artist in the Blind Faith sessions and subsequent Lps, but his recordings with Cream were among rock's most important. Besides redefining the possibilities of the rock guitarists's role, these recordings showcased the perfected Clapton sound. His style, effects and techniques pushed electric guitar into a new dimension. By the end of the '60s, Clapton had given the instrument a new, dynamic and expressive blues/rock voice.

CLAPTON'S GUITARS

Clapton usually played a Fender Telecaster with the Yardbirds. His heavy picking style broke so many strings on the Tele that he earned the name "Slowhand": he would often replace a broken string onstage to the accompaniment of slow, rhythmic handclapping from the band and audience.

With John Mayall's Bluesbreakers he switched to a Gibson Les Paul. With Cream he usually played an SG-shaped Les Paul with a psychedelic paint job; this guitar, played through a stack of Marshall amps, became the standard for countless guitarists. It was the ultimate rock sound throughout the '60s.

With Traffic Clapton alternated between a Gibson ES 335, a Firebird and a Telecaster Custom with a Stratocaster neck. Later he switched to the **Fender** Stratocaster which he still plays today.

CONCERNING NOTATION

In an effort to present a more accessible and comprehensible format in these transcriptions, certain aspects of phrasing have been simplified. You will notice the omission of the obligatory redundant characters in the tab and standard notation. The letters (B for Bend, S for Slides, H for Hammer-on, etc.) have been removed in favor of the graphic symbols alone:

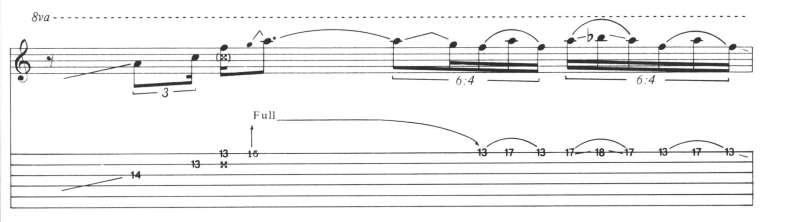

This will yield a two-fold benefit. First, the transcribed score itself will have an uncluttered look which is easier to perceive visually providing a shortcut in the learning process. Second, this format will encourage you, the player, to make the necessary transition from a "tab-only" reader to a guitarist who will begin to relate to standard melodic notation - opening the doors to the worlds of Bach, Paganini, Beethoven, Debussy, Stravinsky and Coltrane. In this format, the laws of common sense will prevail. The following phrase will serve to illustrate the logic of this less cumbersome notation:

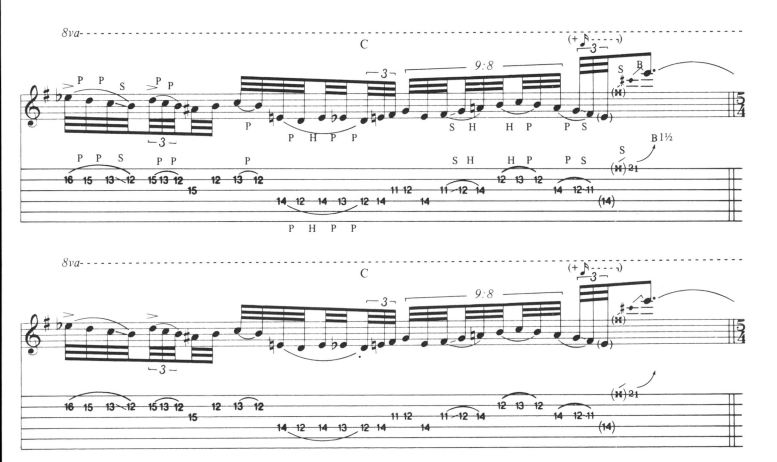

LEGEND

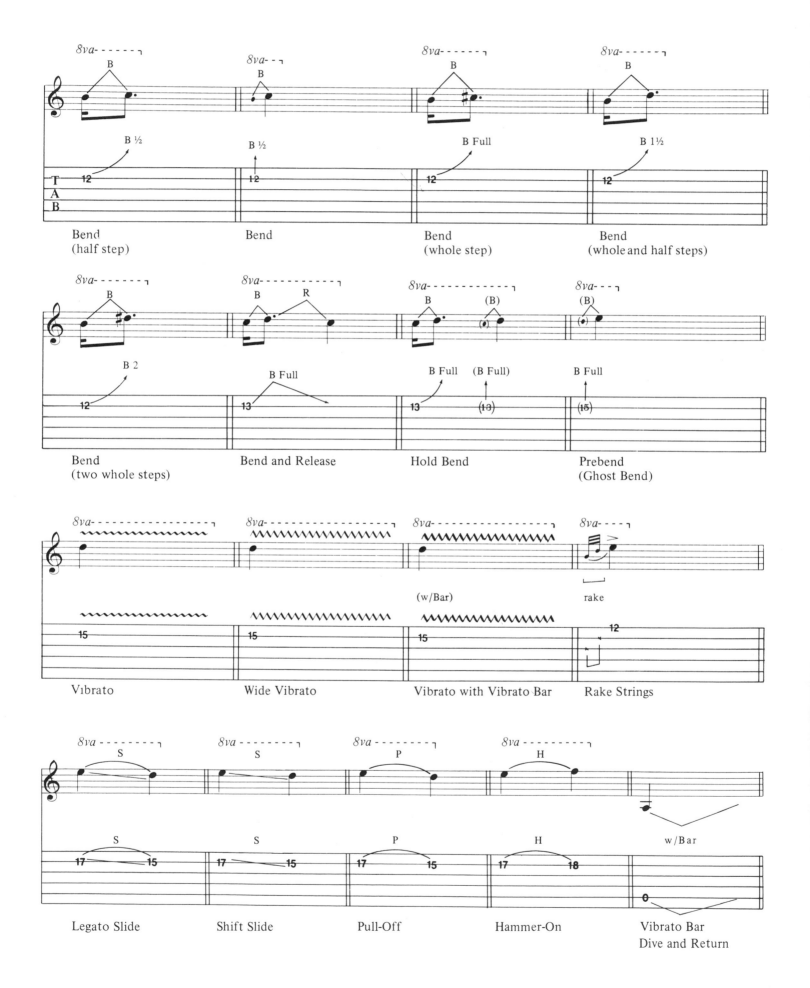

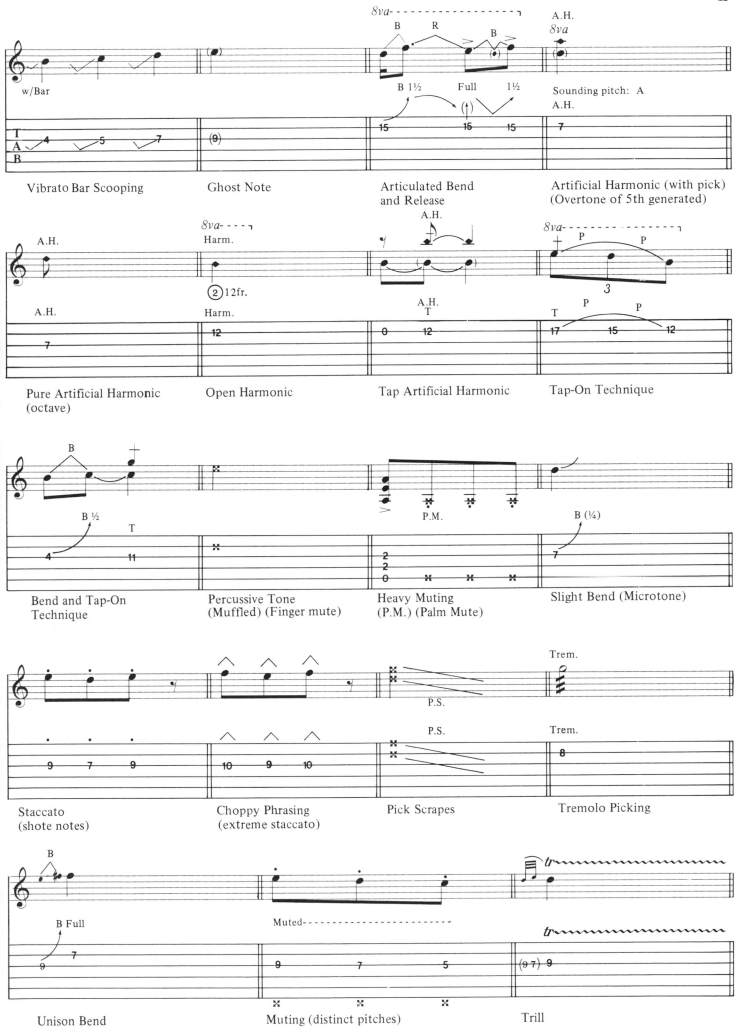

Vibrato Bar Scooping

Ghost Note

Articulated Bend and Release

Artificial Harmonic (with pick) (Overtone of 5th generated)

Pure Artificial Harmonic (octave)

Open Harmonic

Tap Artificial Harmonic

Tap-On Technique

Bend and Tap-On Technique

Percussive Tone (Muffled) (Finger mute)

Heavy Muting (P.M.) (Palm Mute)

Slight Bend (Microtone)

Staccato (shote notes)

Choppy Phrasing (extreme staccato)

Pick Scrapes

Tremolo Picking

Unison Bend

Muting (distinct pitches)

Trill

BOOM BOOM

Words and Music by
JOHN LEE HOOKER

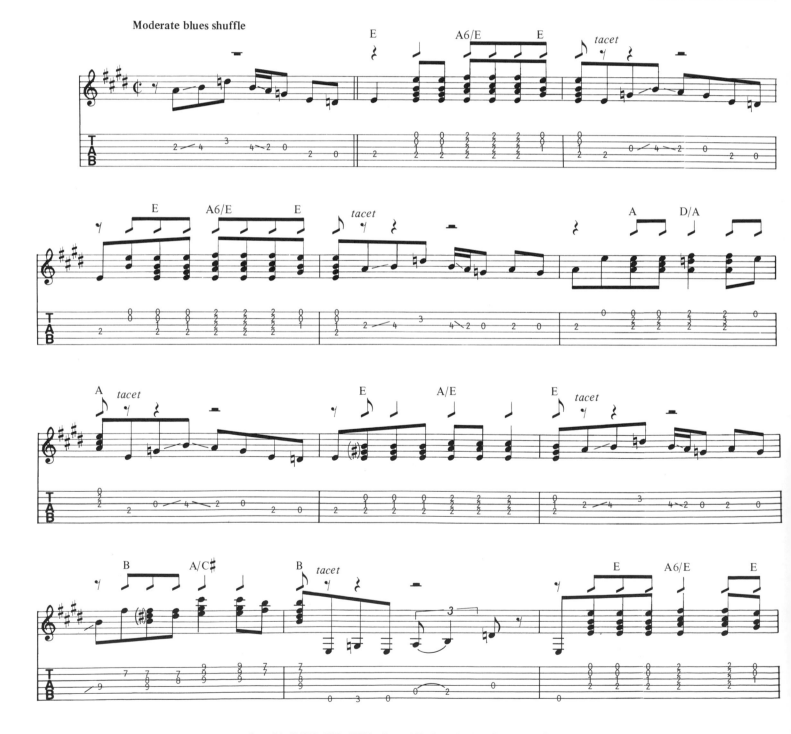

HONEY IN YOUR HIPS

Words and Music by
KEITH REIF

Moderate Bo Diddley beat

When I get out on the

I want you and-a you want me.

We're gon-na dance all night 'til we both feel free.

We'll shake and we shim-my right a-

cross the floor.

BABY WHAT'S WRONG

Words and Music by
JIMMY REED

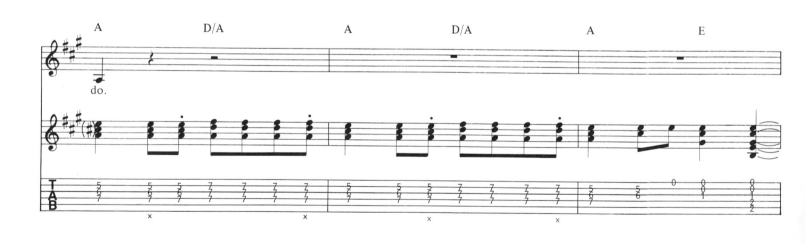

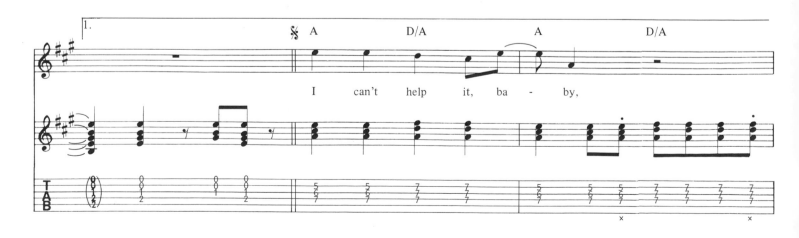

I WISH YOU WOULD

Words and Music by
BILLY BOY ARNOLD

D.S. al Coda
Repeat 12 times

You know, ba - by, that I love you so.___

You know, pret - ty ba - by, it hurts ___ me to see you go.___

Wo, ___ yeah.

Oh ___ yeah.___

(Harp solo)

Repeat and fade

A CERTAIN GIRL

Words and Music by
NAOMI NEVILLE

D.S. 𝄋 *(1st verse, play*
1st ending, take repeat)
al Coda

Tacet

3. Well, I've a

CODA

tell ya. *(No!)*   I can't   tell ya. *(No!)*   I can't   tell ya.*(No!)*   I can't   tell ya.

GOOD MORNING LITTLE SCHOOL GIRL

Words and Music by
DON LEVEL and BOB LOVE

If you let me, I can tease you you ba - by.
to the mu - sic of the rock and roll,___ oh.
Tell your sis - ters and your broth - er that I love you.

Hey, hey___

hey hey hey,___ hey h - hey hey.___ Hey, yeah.

All slides performed
w/ bottleneck

Hey,___ hey hey hey.___

I AIN'T GOT YOU

Words and Music by
CALVIN CARTER

four, for-ty-four.   I got a   mo-jo,   yeah,   don't   you   know?_   I'm

all   dressed   up   with   no   place   to   go.   I've got   No,   I   ain't   got   you.

FOR YOUR LOVE

Words and Music by
GRAHAM GOULDMAN

For your love.

To Coda

tacet

Slow rock beat

(Drums only)

For your love,—

for your love,— I would give the— stars— a-bove.—

For your love,— for your love,— I would

give you all I could.——

D. C. al Coda

CODA

For your love.——

Oooh.)

GOT TO HURRY

By OSCAR RASPUTIN

Resume 12-bar rhythm guitar pattern (as in 1st 12 bars)

Resume 12-bar rhythm guitar

LONELY YEARS

Words and Music by
JOHN MAYALL

Slow blues shuffle
Open A Tuning

All slides performed w/bottleneck

Prais - es to the wine_____ from the salt of_____ all__ my

tears.

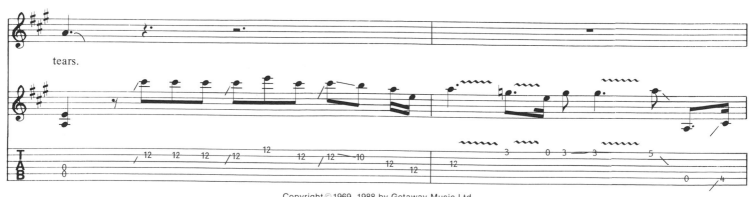

I'll be meet-ing lot-ta peo-ple._____ I got-ta start now__ and fig-ure out my

time.

I got-ta vis-it lot-ta peo-ple,_____ I got-ta start now__ and fig-ure out my

time. I be-lieve with a feel-in',_____

I got-ta move_____ on down the line.

BERNARD JENKINS

By ERIC CLAPTON

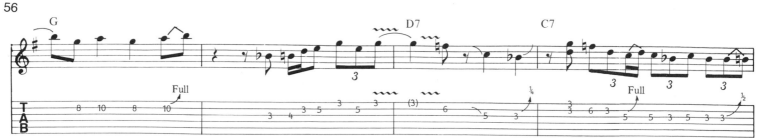

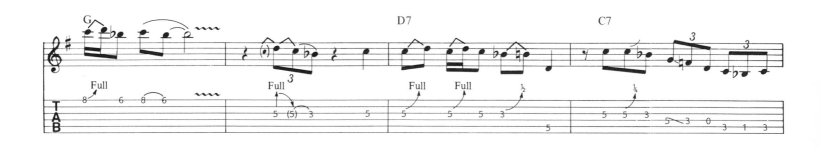
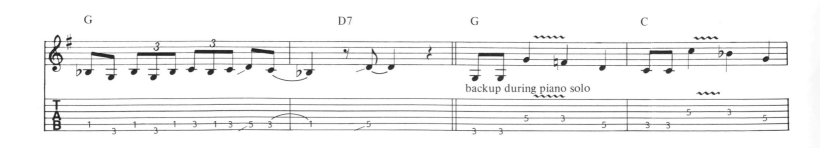
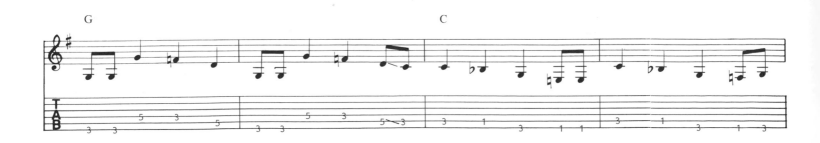

HIDEAWAY

Words and Music by
FREDDY KING and SONNY THOMPSON

ALL YOUR LOVE

Words and Music by
OTIS RUSH

Repeat previous 12-bar pattern.

2nd guitar plays lead part of the following choruses.

ba - by,__ I nev - er knew what I was miss - in',__

Hey, hey, ba - miss - in'.__

Repeat 2nd guitar part as in beginning instrumental.

RAMBLIN' ON MY MIND

By ROBERT JOHNSON
Arranged by ERIC CLAPTON

Slow blues shuffle

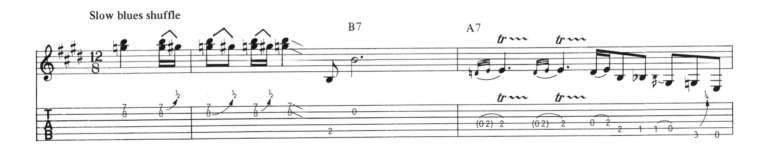

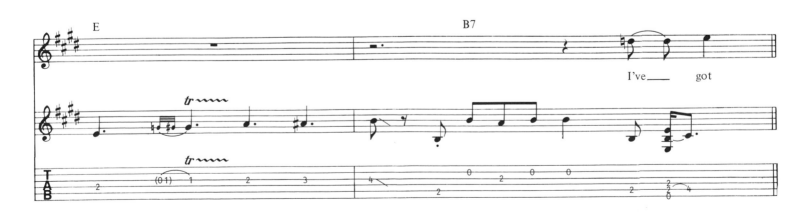

I've___ got

HAVE YOU EVER LOVED A WOMAN

Words and Music by
BILLY MYLES

Have you ev-er loved a wom-an____ so much you real - ly_____ hate to be a -

lone? ____

Have you ev-er loved a wom-an____ so much you real - ly____ hate to be a -

lone?____

feedback

When all_ the time you know_____ that lit-tle girl, li'l' girl,___ well, done you_

And the part that hurts you bad, ___

when you nev-er, well, you nev-er ___ gon-na see her a-

gain. ___

Have you ev - er loved a wom-an____ so much it real-ly, real-ly____ hurts to be a-

WRAPPING PAPER

Words and Music by
JACK BRUCE and PETER BROWN

Moderate, light shuffle

(1st time only, guitar tacet)

1. Wrap-ping pa-per   in the gut-ter   mov-ing slow-ly
2. In the cit-y,   feel-ing pret-ty   down and out and mak-ing
3. Some-day I'll get back,   some-how I'll do it.   I'll ar-rive there and

as the wind on the sea   (Fac-es call-ing,   rain's mov-ing.)
love to you on the shore   (Mov-ing build-ings,   fac-es emp-ty.)
you'll be there to meet me.   (All to-geth-er,   tread the weeds down.)

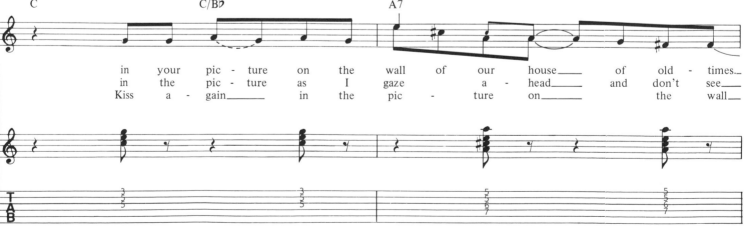

in your pic-ture on the wall of our house of old-times.
in the pic-ture as I gaze a-head and don't see
Kiss a-gain in the pic-ture on the wall

(Can you hear me?) Can you hear me (Can you hear me?) won-der-ing sad - ly?
(That they're call-ing,) that they're call - ing, (that they're call-ing.) won-der-ing sad - ly.
(Where I loved you,) in the old house, (where I loved you.) loved you so well.

Instrumental

Oooh, ooh,

Repeat previous 12-bar rhythm guitar part

Fade up w/ volume pedal

Full   Full

Fade, 3rd time

Shat - tered win- dows.

Full   Full   1½   Full   Full

stairs to walk up. Ooh

I FEEL FREE

Words and Music by
JACK BRUCE and PETE BROWN

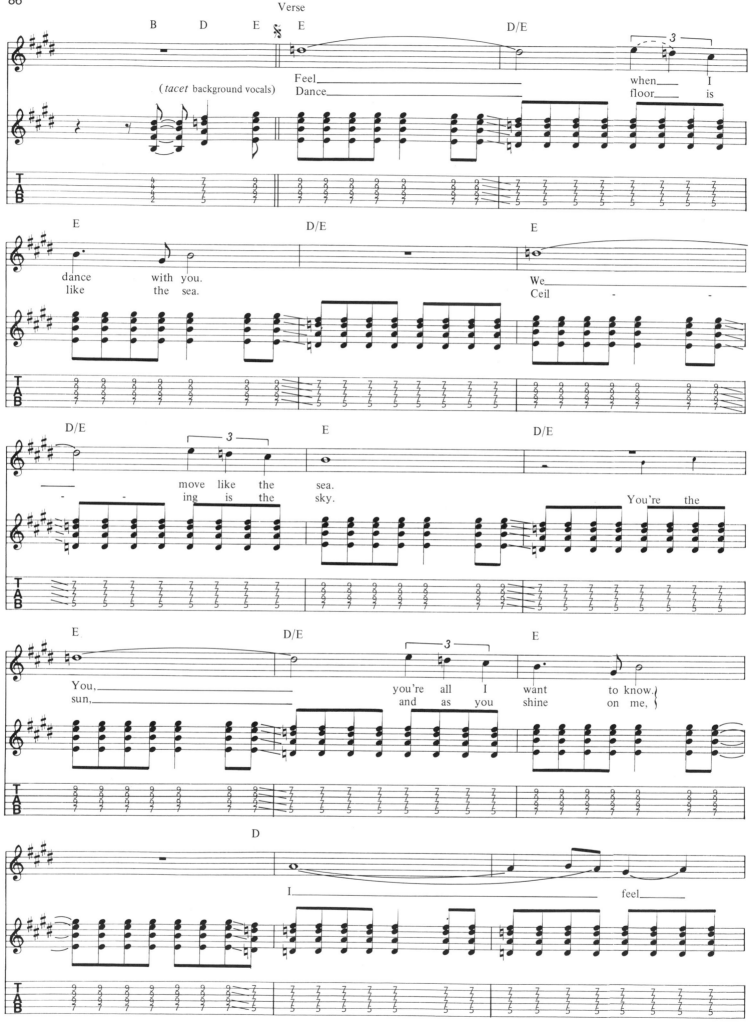

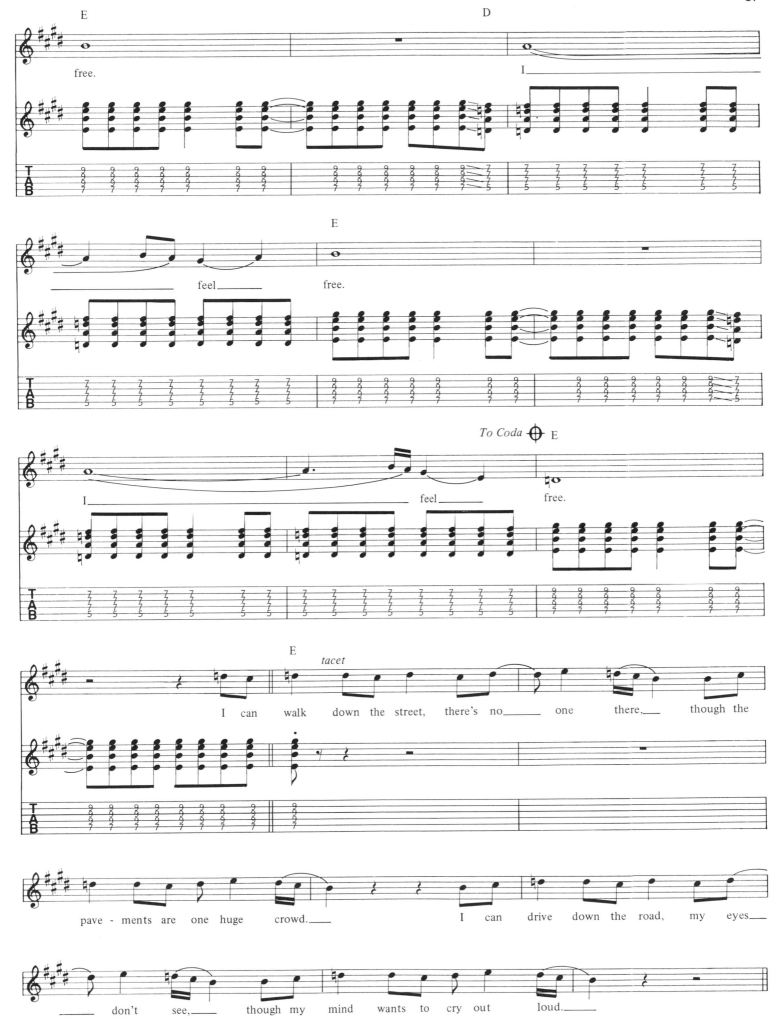

SPOONFUL

Words and Music by
WILLIE DIXON

Ev'ry-thing's a - fight-in' a-bout it, uh— Ev-'ry-thing's a-

cry - in' a - bout it_____ uh Ev-'ry-thing's a, ev-'ry-thing's a-

die - in' a-bout it. Ev-'ry-thing's a - cry - in' a - bout it. Ev-'ry-thing's a-

ly - in' a-bout it._____ Li'l' old,____ li'l' old,_____

spoon - ful,___ spoon - ful._____

LAWDY MAMA

Traditional
Arranged by ERIC CLAPTON

STRANGE BREW

Words and Music by ERIC CLAPTON,
FELIX PAPPALARDI and MIKE COLLINS

Moderate Funk/Rock

don't watch out,___ it - 'll stick to you, to you.___

What kind of fool are you?___

On a
boat in the mid -dle of the rag-ing___ sea,___ she would
make a scene___ for it all to be ig - nored,___
and would-n't you be bored.___

SUNSHINE OF YOUR LOVE

Words and Music by JACK BRUCE,
PETER BROWN and ERIC CLAPTON

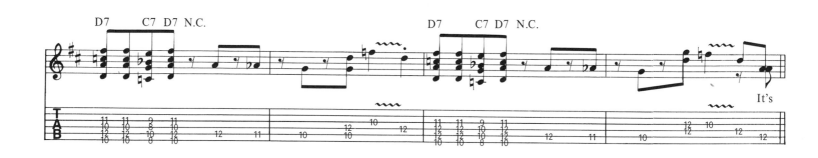

TALES OF BRAVE ULYSSES

Words and Music by
ERIC CLAPTON and MARTIN SHARP

Moderate rock beat

thought the lead - en win - ter would bring you down for - ev - er, but you

rode up - on a steam - er to the vio - lence of the sun.___

Wah wah on lead guitar only

And the
Her

D   C   G/B   B♭   D   C   C/B   B♭

Ti - ny pur - ple fish - es run laugh - ing through your fin - gers, and you

Rhythm guitar tacet

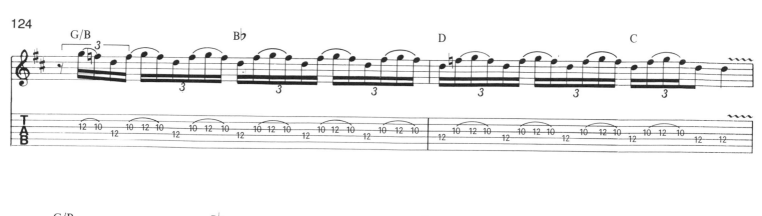

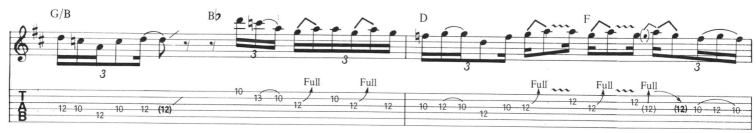

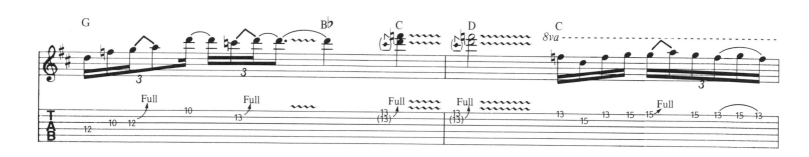

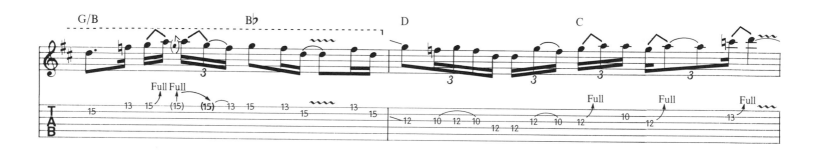

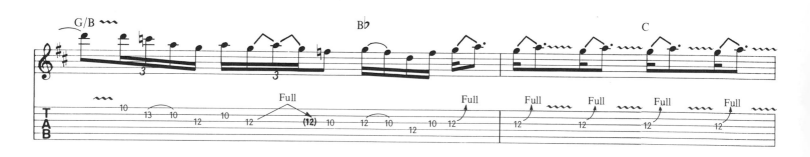

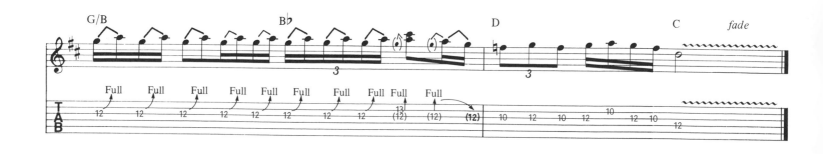

STEPPIN' OUT

Words and Music by
JAMES BRACKEN

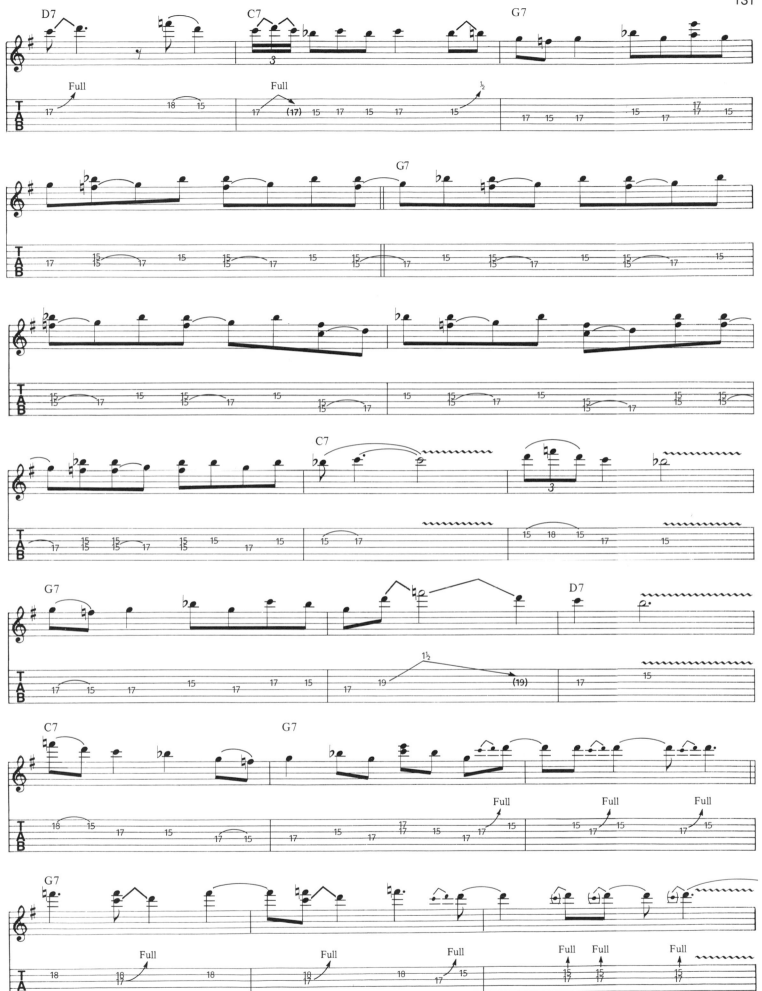

ANYONE FOR TENNIS

Words and Music by
ERIC CLAPTON and MARTIN SHARPE

Bright country two-beat

(Mellotron and acoustic strumming guitar)

Twice up-on a time,___ in the val -
Ice creams are all melt - ing on the streets___

- ley of the tears,___ the auc-tion-eer is bid-ding for a
- of blood-y beer,___ while the beg-gars stain the pave-ments with fluo -

box of fad - ing years. And the el-e-phants are danc - ing on the
res - cent Christ-mas cheer. And the Bent-ley driv-ing gu - ru is

graves of squeal-ing mice. An-y-one___ for ten - nis?
put-ting up his price.

Would-n't that___ be___ nice? (Mellotron)
And the

WHITE ROOM

Words and Music by
JACK BRUCE and PETER BROWN

Guitar Solo

CROSSROADS

Words and Music by
ERIC CLAPTON

I went down

Muted

D. S. 𝄋 (3rd verse) al Coda

BADGE

Words and Music by
ERIC CLAPTON and GEORGE HARRISON

Talk - in' 'bout a girl that looks__ quite like you.

She did - n't have the time to wait__ in the queue.__

She cried a - way her life since she fell off the cra - dle.

PRESENCE OF THE LORD

Words and Music by
ERIC CLAPTON

Slow rock ballad

I have fin-'lly found a {way / place} to live

just like I nev-er could be-fore.

I know that I don't have
(And I know I don't have

CAN'T FIND MY WAY HOME

Words and Music by
STEVE WINWOOD

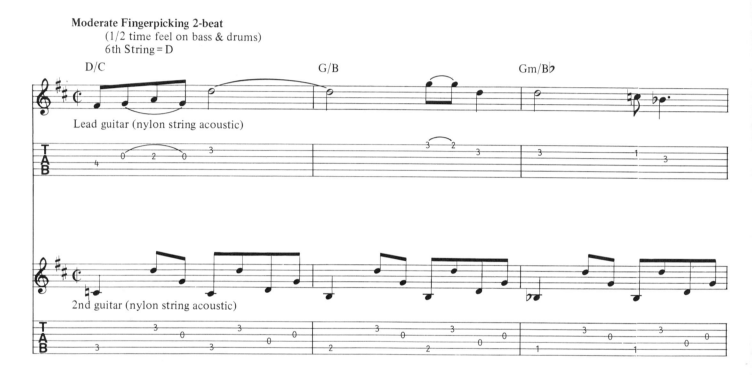

wast - ed___ and I can't___ find my way home.

Oooh,_____ but I__

can't   find   my____ way____ home.

SLEEPING IN THE GROUND

Words and Music by
SAM MYERS